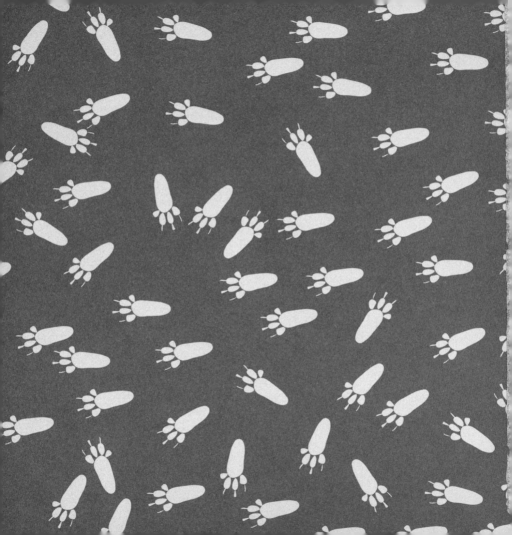

WHEN MEERKATS TURN BAD

WHEN MEERKATS TURN BAD

Summersdale Publishers Ltd
46 West Street
Chichester
West Sussex
PO19 1RP
UK

www.summersdale.com

Printed and bound in Czech Republic

ISBN: 978-1-84953-231-0

Images pp. 6-75 ® Shutterstock, pp.76-93 ® iStockphoto

Substantial discounts on bulk quantities of Summersdale books are available to corporations, professional associations and other organisations. For details telephone Summersdale Publishers on (+44-1243-771107), fax (+44-1243-786300) or email (nicky@summersdale.com).

WHEN MEERKATS TURN BAD

summersdale

INTRODUCTION

To many the concept of misbehaving meerkats is totally alien. But secret new footage has now revealed the real reason why meerkats are so jittery.

Cute and cuddly? Or cunning and undercover? That's what we set out to discover.

Prepare to be horrified as we plunge into a world of sexual hi-jinks, prurient peeping and general common-or-garden depravity.

With unprecedented access to the truth behind these creatures we've come to know and love, take a look at the obscene, debauched and downright sordid things that can happen when meerkats turn bad...

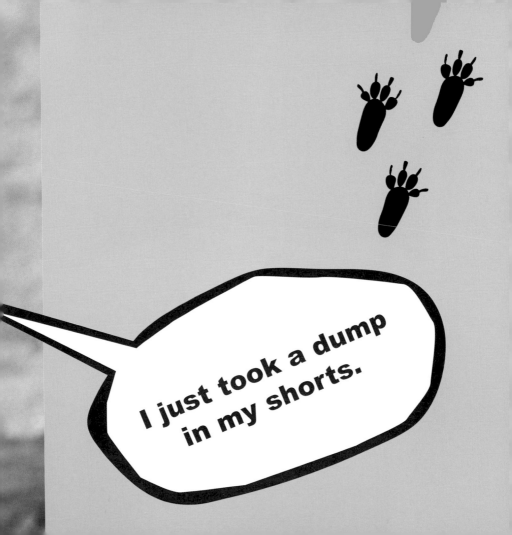

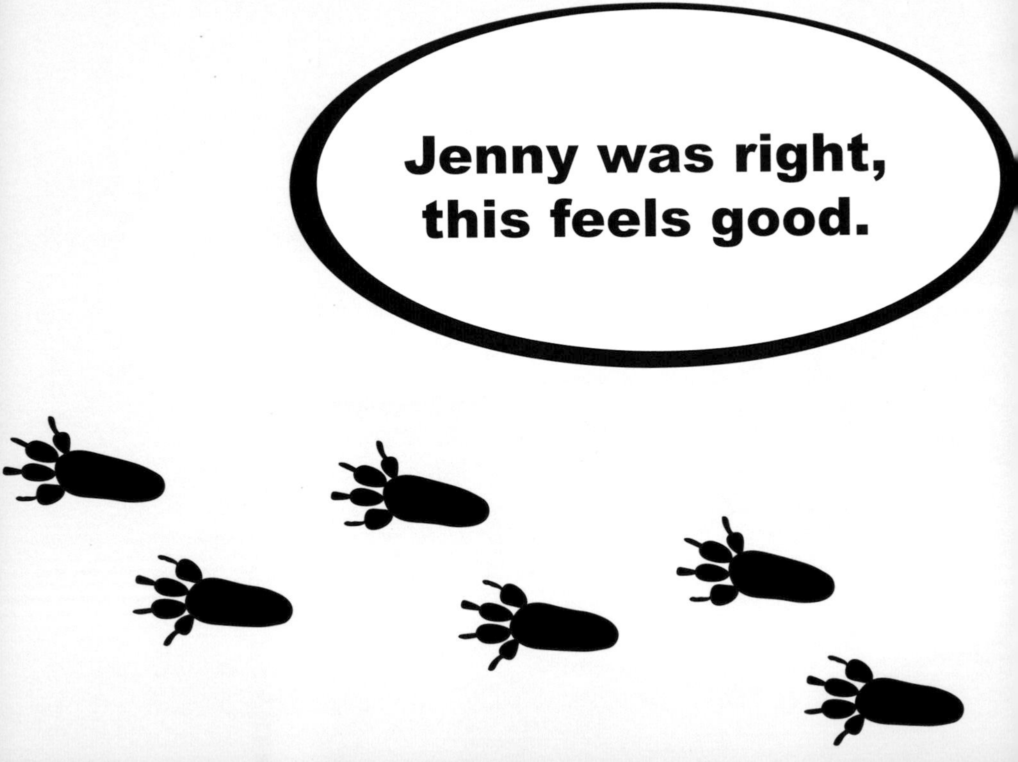
Jenny was right, this feels good.

I'll be submissive! Now what's our safe word?

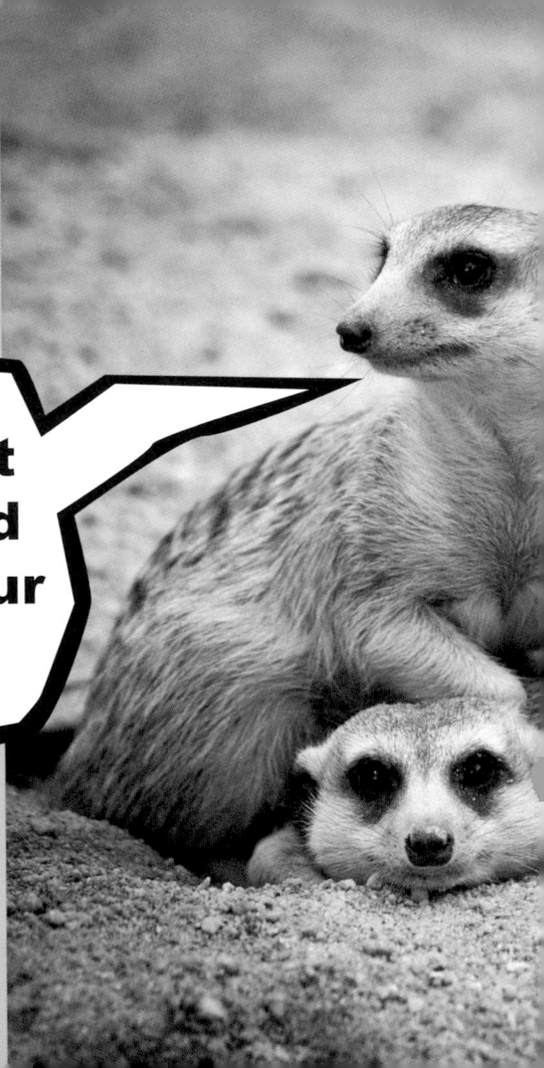
And I brought back his head as a sign of our VICTORY!

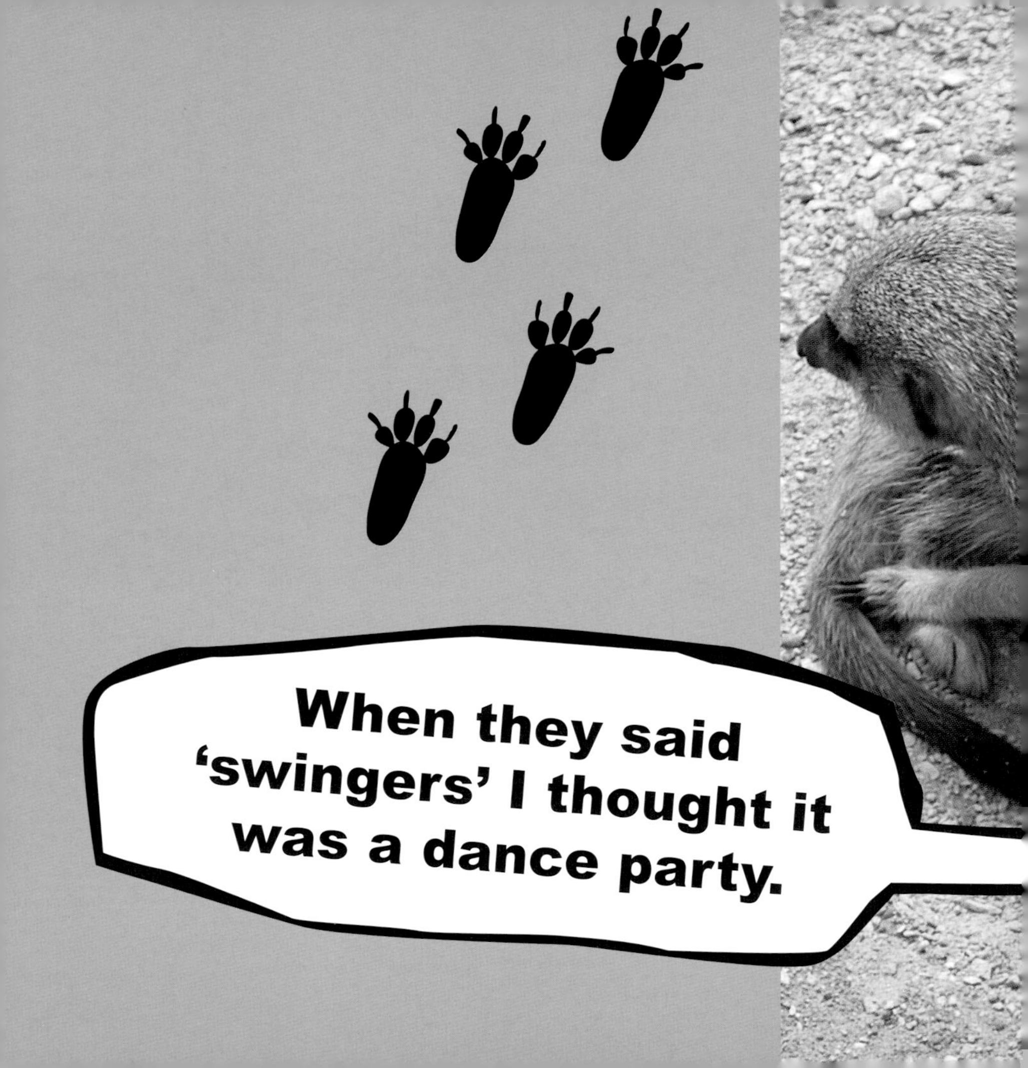
When they said 'swingers' I thought it was a dance party.

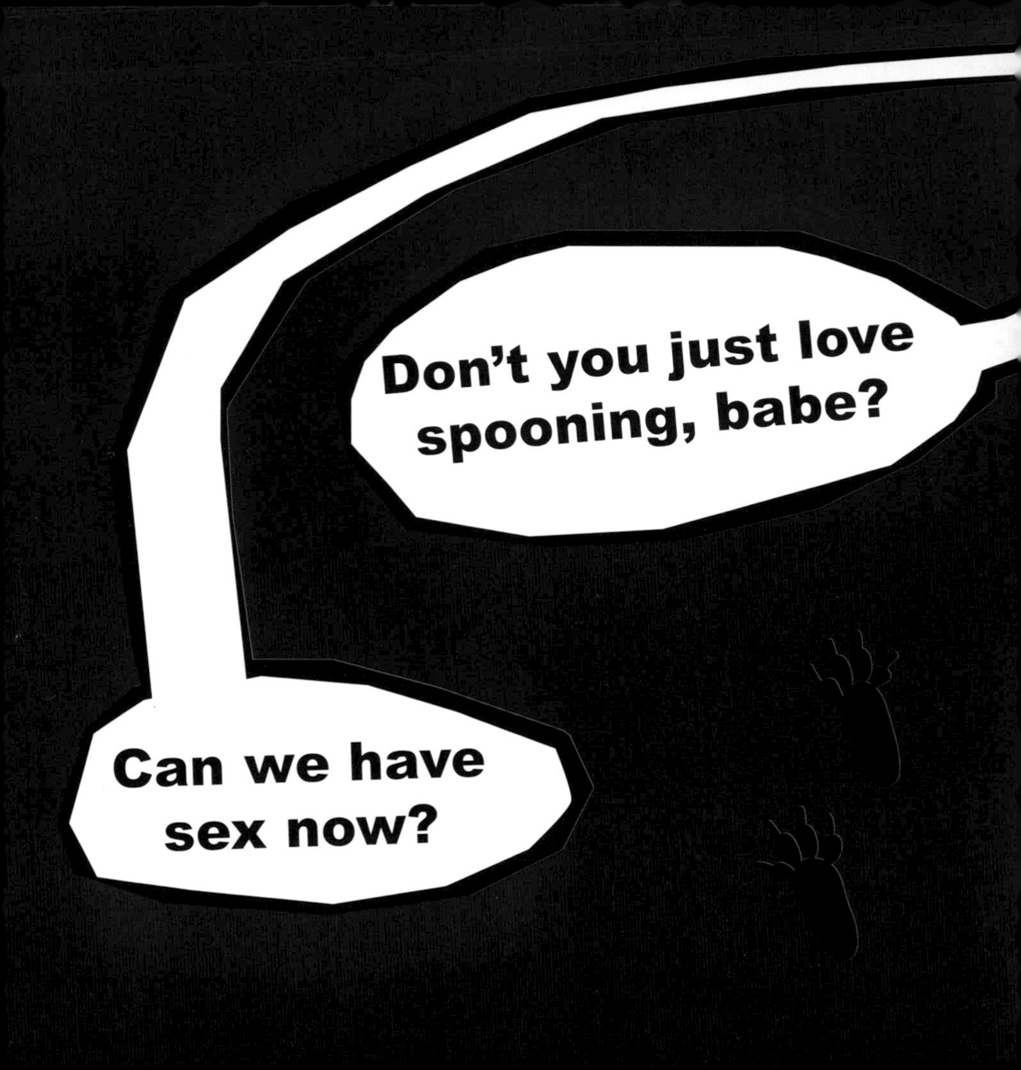
Don't you just love spooning, babe?
Can we have sex now?

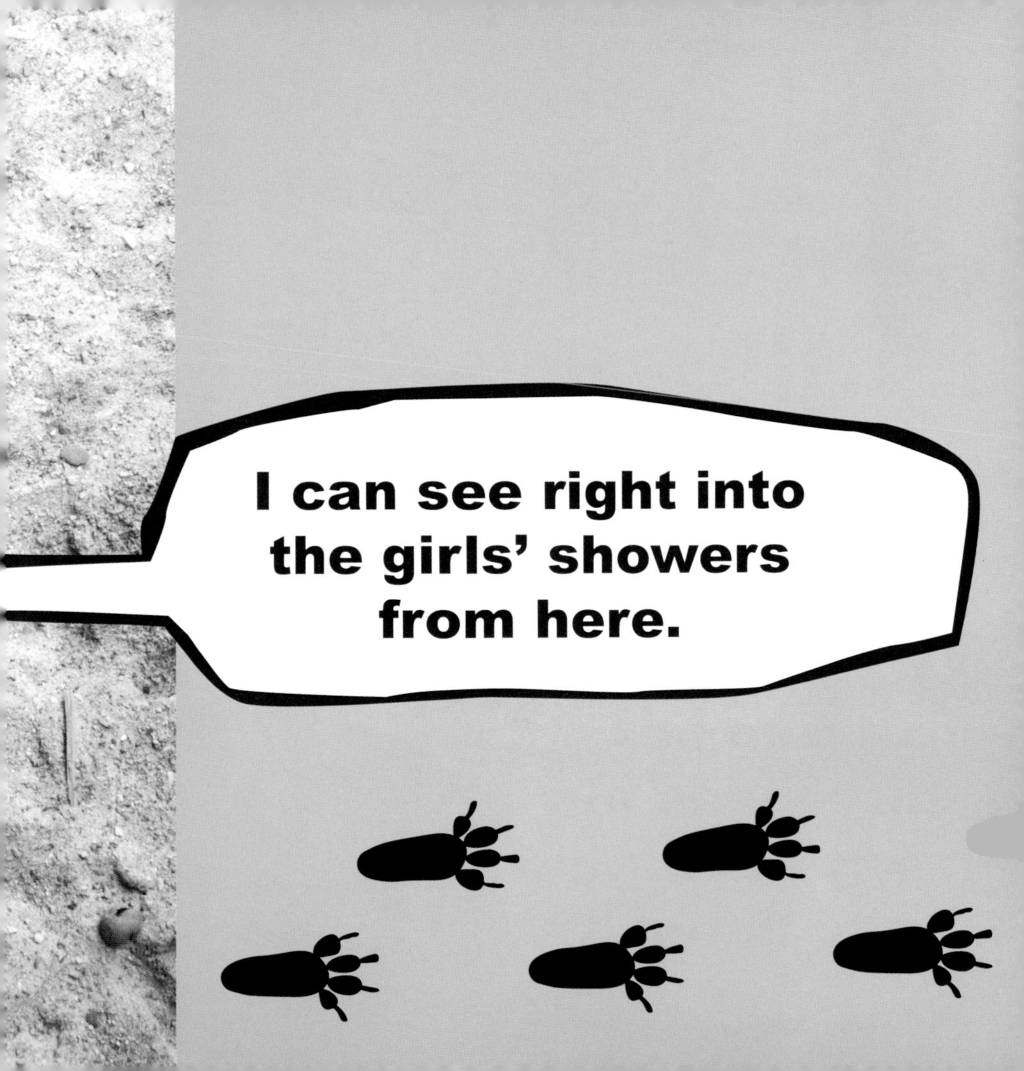
I can see right into the girls' showers from here.

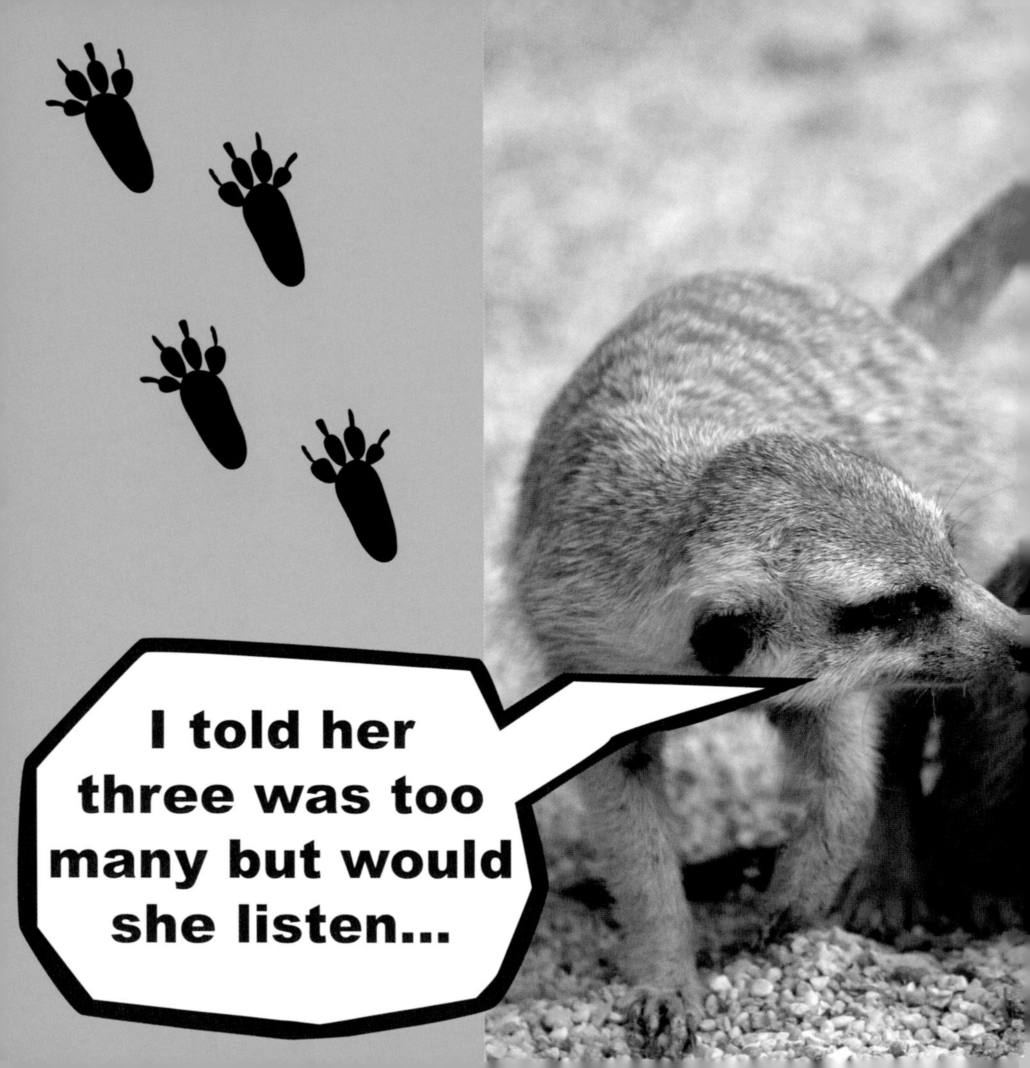
I told her three was too many but would she listen...

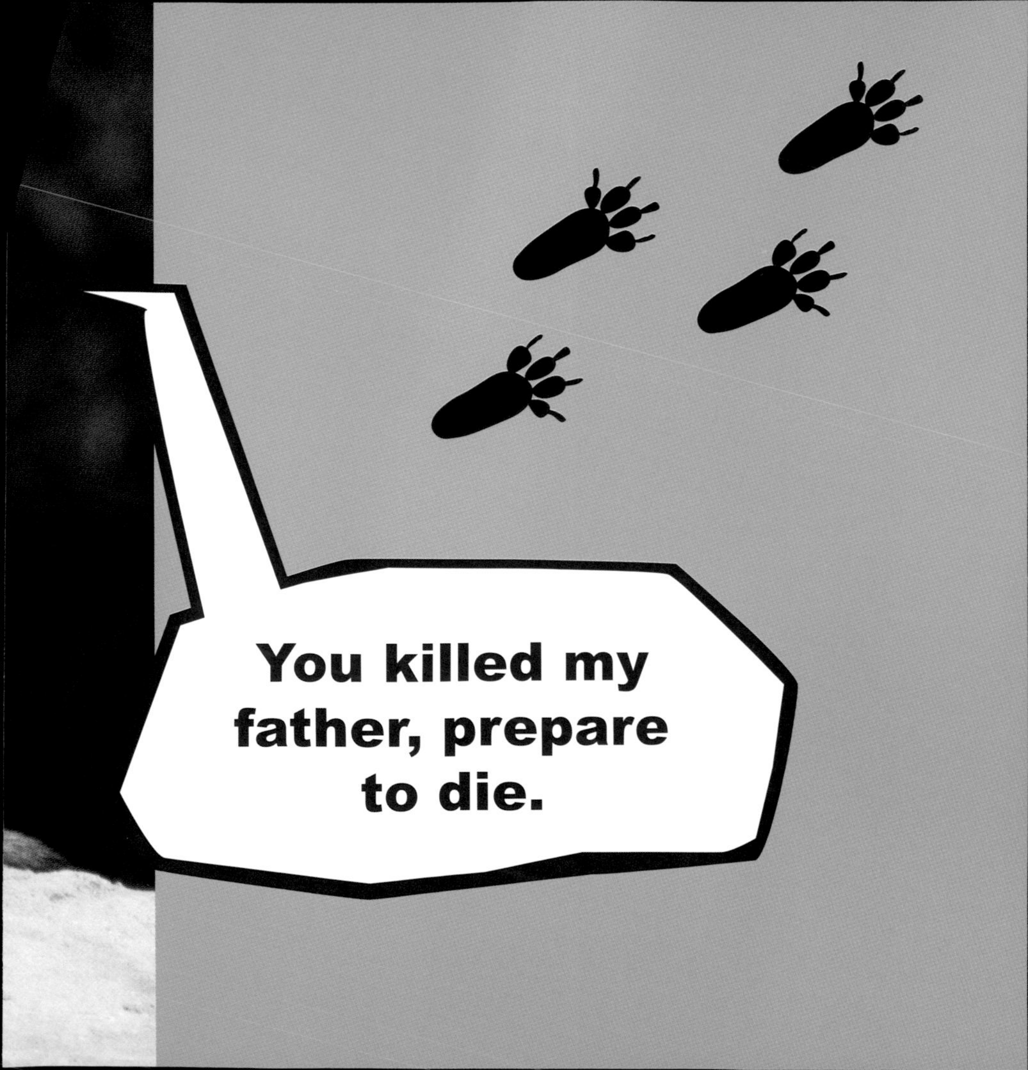
You killed my father, prepare to die.

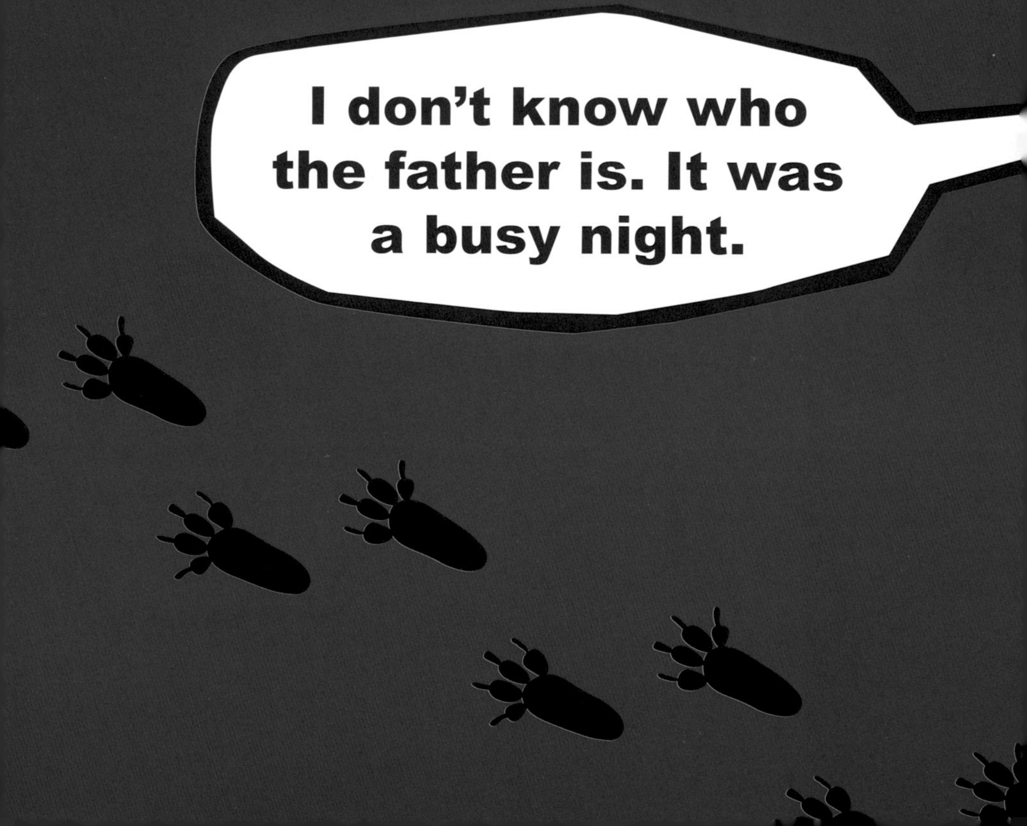
I don’t know who the father is. It was a busy night.

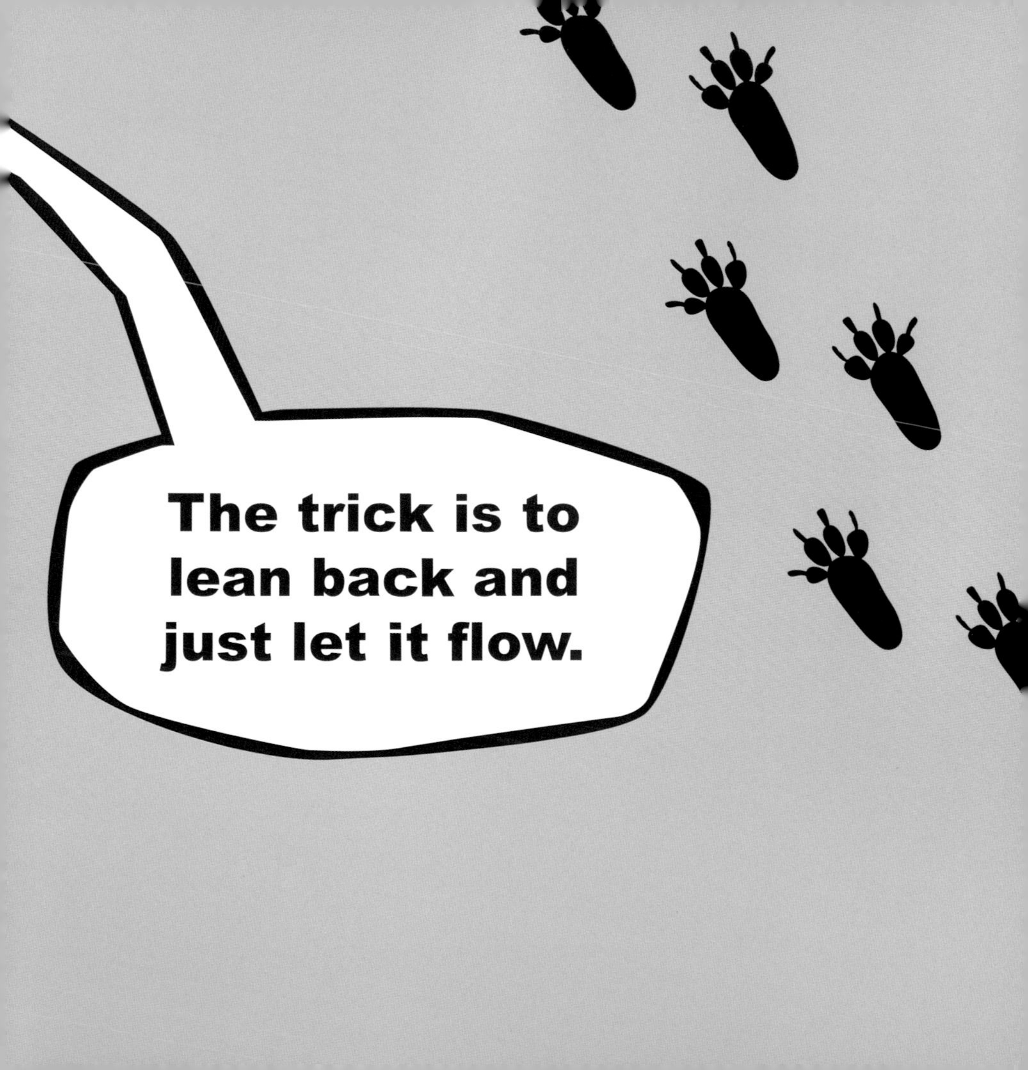
The trick is to lean back and just let it flow.

When is someone going to invent pockets?

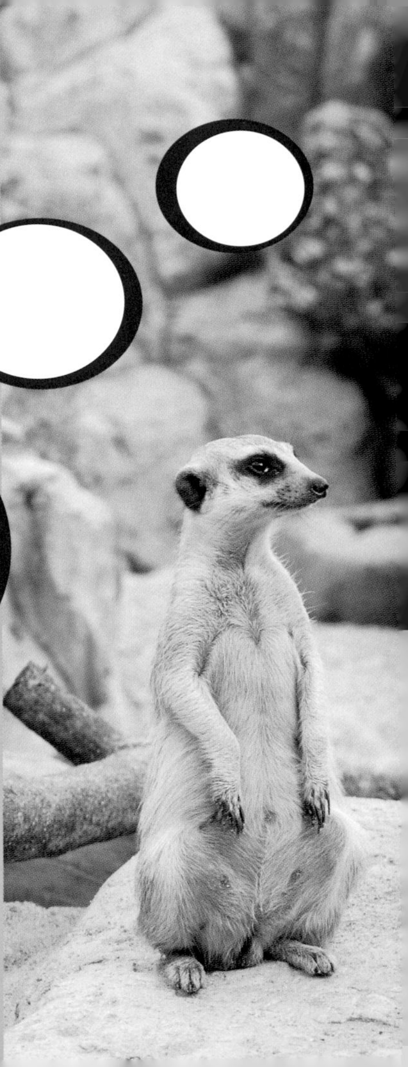

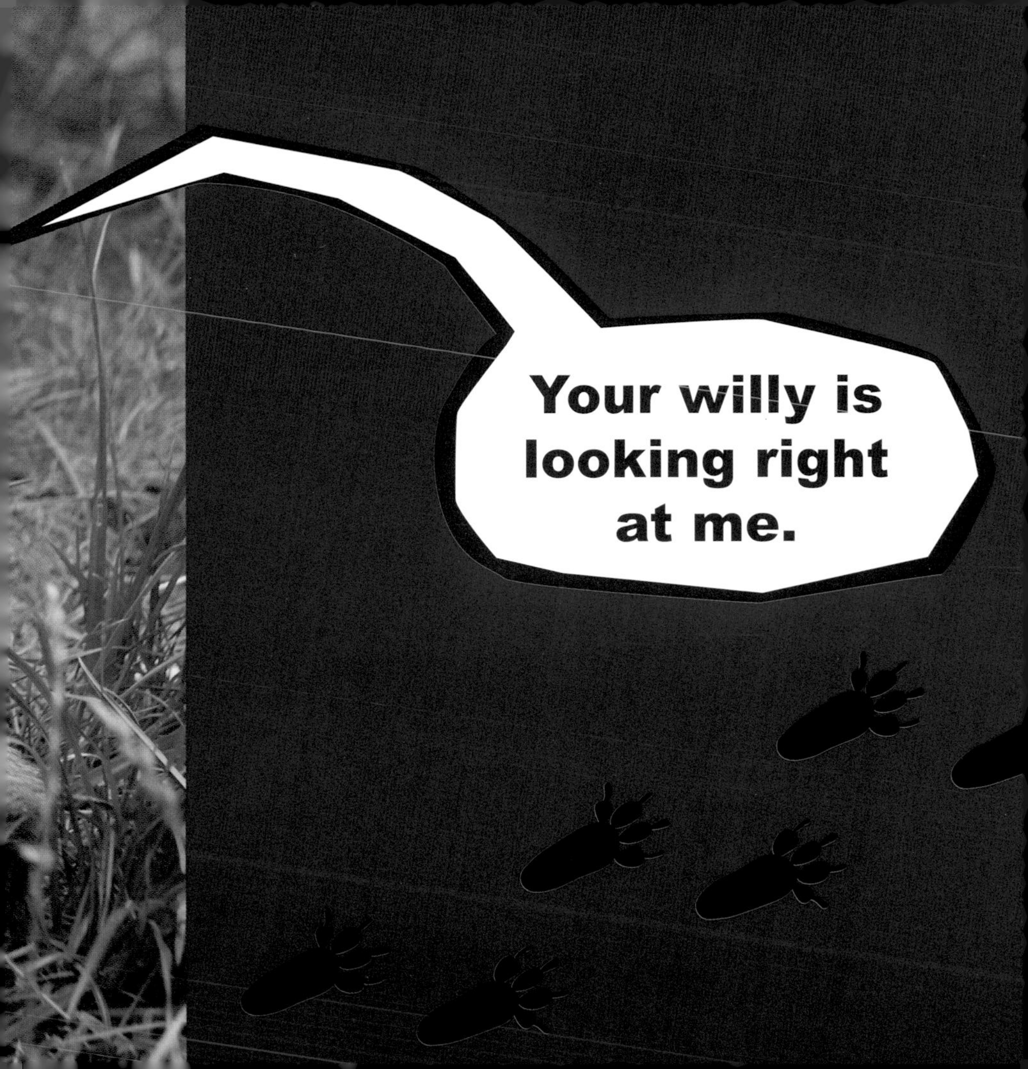
Your willy is looking right at me.

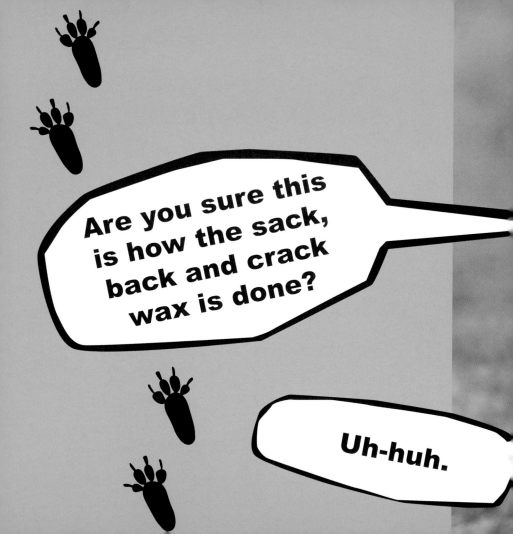

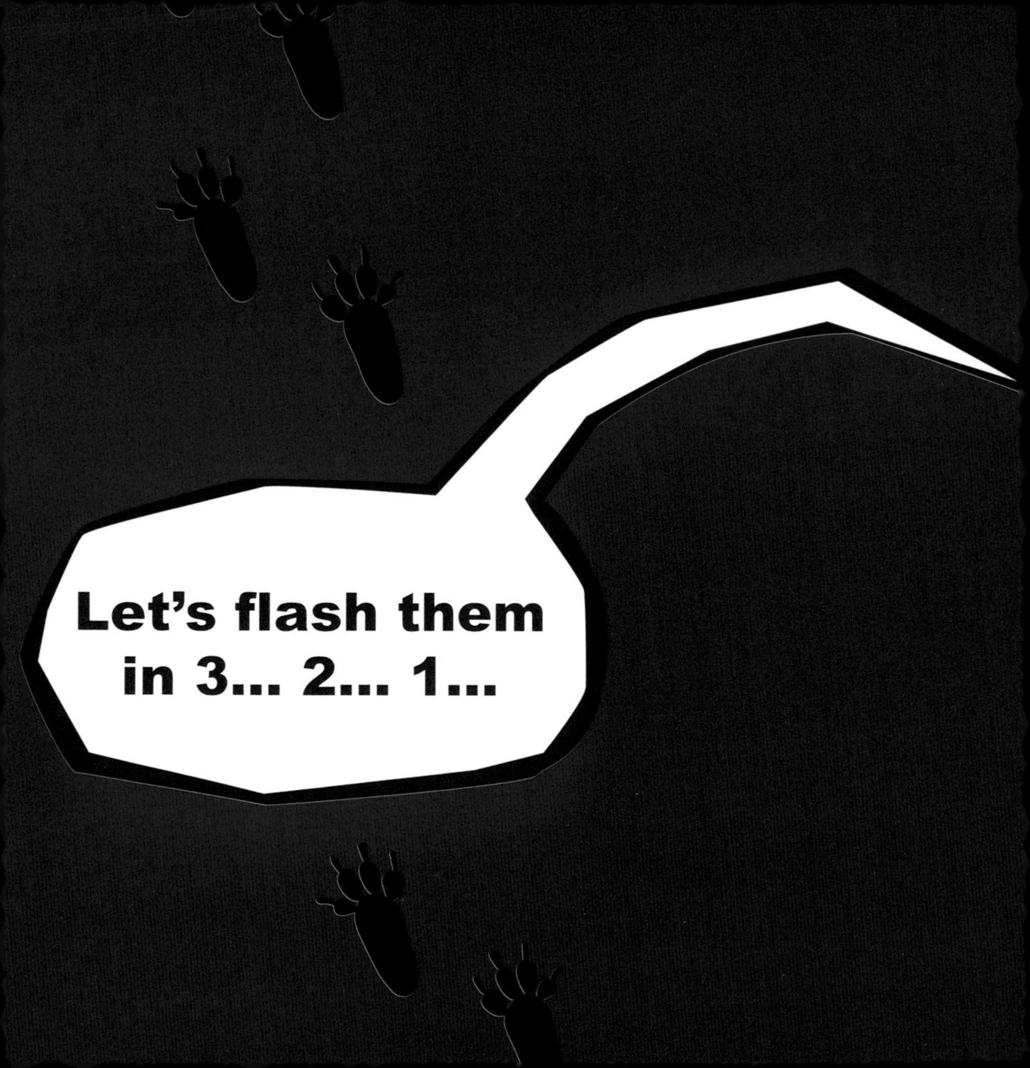
Let’s flash them
in 3… 2… 1…

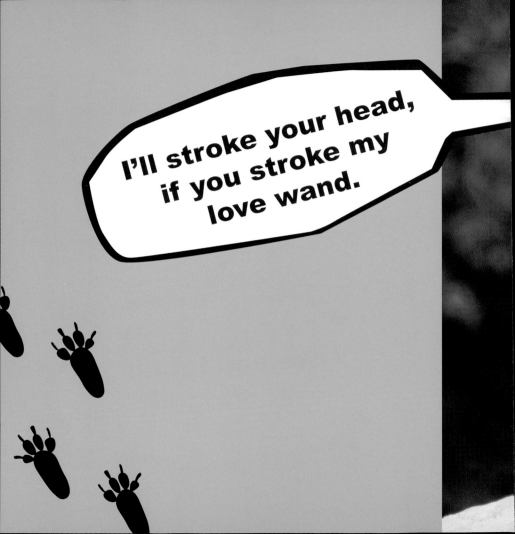

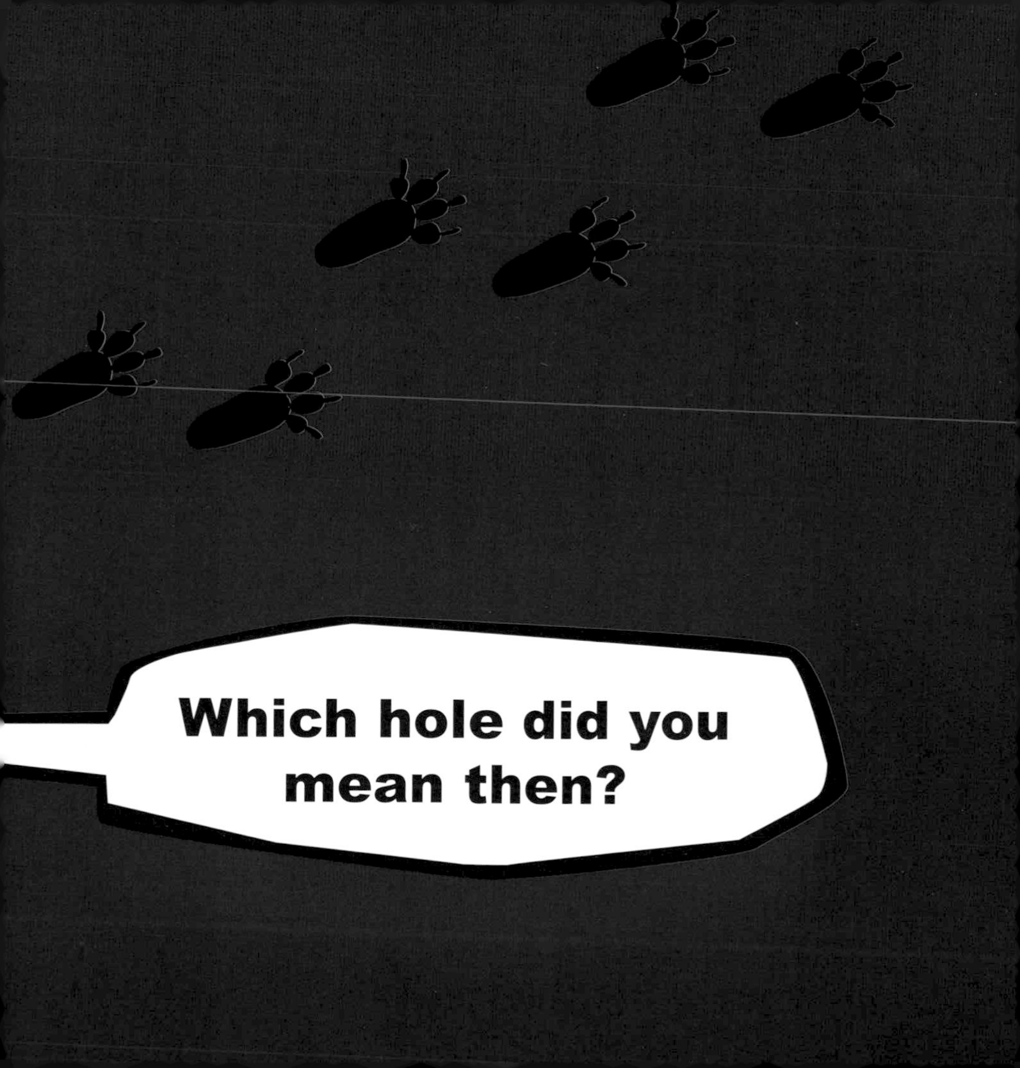
Which hole did you mean then?

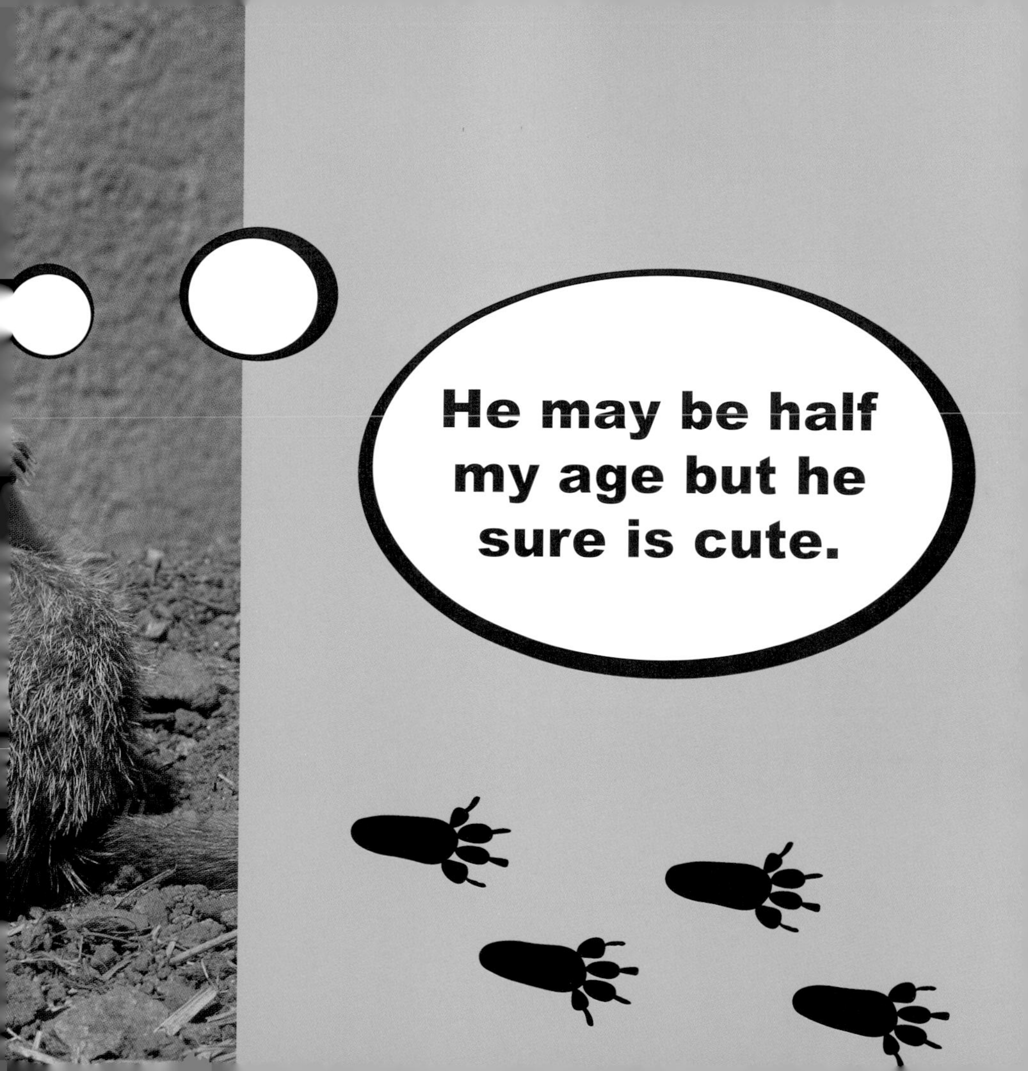
He may be half my age but he sure is cute.

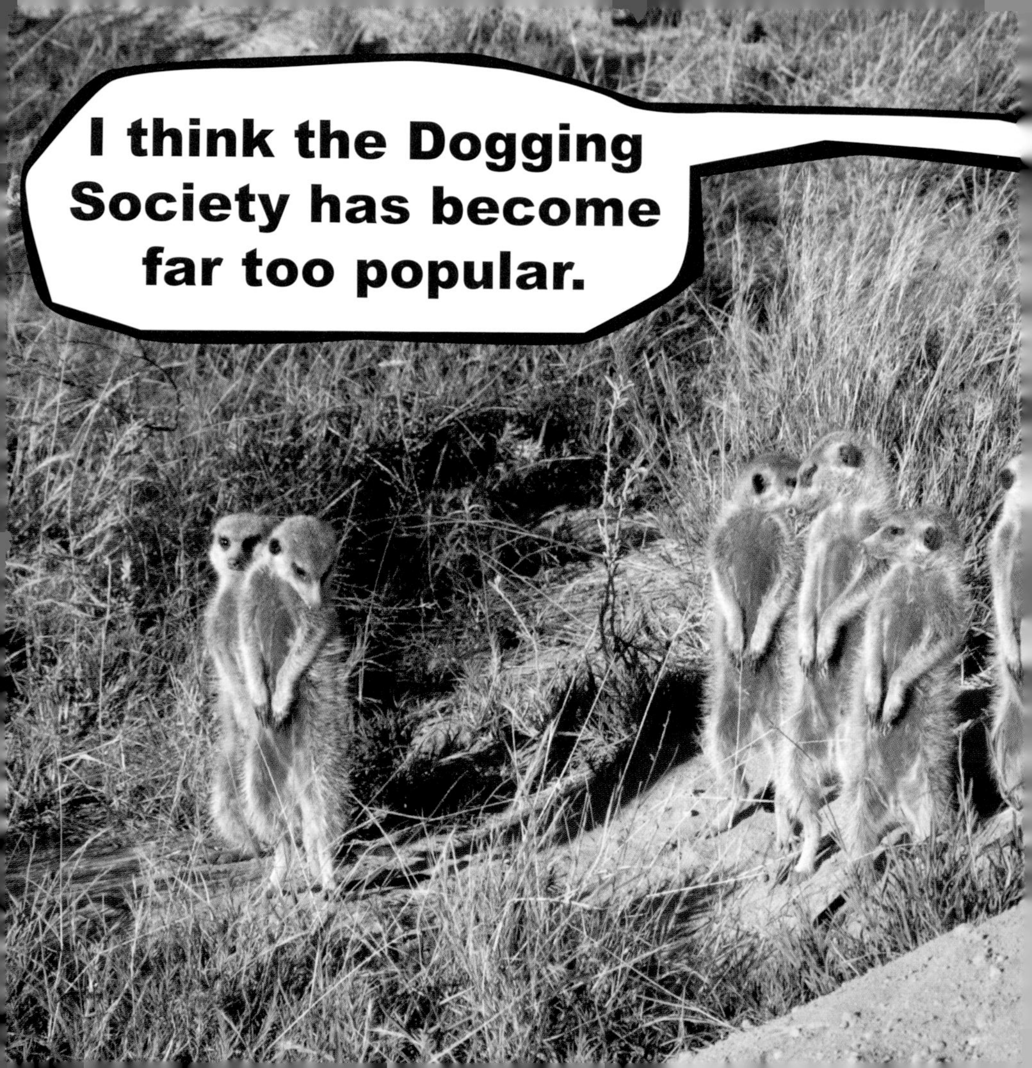
I think the Dogging Society has become far too popular.

Photo Credits

I just took a dump	lightpoet
Look I can't go	Francois Etienne du Plessis
Whose foot is that	Tratong
Jenny was right	Dragon_fang
I'll be submissive	Mlorenz
And I brought back his head	Tratong
I took a Viagra	Henk Bentlage
When they said swingers	Timothy Craig Lubcke
That'll teach me to have a vindaloo	Sarah Cates
Don't you just love spooning	Carol Coolahan
I can see right into the girls' showers	Kristina Stasiuliene
I told her three was too many	Tina Rencelj
Fancy a shag?	Miodrag Nejkovic
Does my bum look big in this?	Henk Bentlage
If anyone asks	Gracious_tiger
What? Oh yeah, I wax my chest	Trevor Kelly
You killed my father	Maria Gioberti
Check out my Brazilian	Holger Ehlers
You think that's my tail	David W Crippen
I don't know who the father is	Defpicture
The trick is to lean back	Wouter Tolenaars
When is someone going to invent pockets?	Behindlens
Psst – I got watches	Jon le-bon
How you doin'?	Colette3
Your willy is looking right at me	MariusdeGraf
Loo roll's run out	Elina Ryzhenkova
This place sucks	Dwphotos
Are you sure this how…?	EcoPrint
That'll teach us to experiment	James R. Hearn
Let's flash them in 3, 2, 1	Kristina Stasiuliene
Are you looking at me, pal?	Ethylalkohol
I'll stroke your head	Maria Gioberti
Threesome!	Dwphotos
OK, ten paces then turn and shoot	Fotomicar
Which hole did you mean then?	Dean bertoncelj
I see a little silhouetto	Jeryl Tan
He may be half my age	Soile Berg
Eyes to the wall	Peter Malsbury
Voulez-vous?	Gaspare Messina
Weed	Kevdog818
How old did you say you were?	Jonathan Heger
What happened last night?	Henk Bentlage
Dogging Society	Peter Malsbury
Yes! Spank me harder	Vladimir Raus.

www.summersdale.com